OH NO! I'VE TURNED INTO MY MOTHER: A Let's Read Together Book © copyright 2025 by Jay Forte. All rights reserved. No part of this book may be reproduced in any form whatsoever, by photography or xerography or by any other means, by broadcast or transmission, by translation into any kind of language, nor by recording electronically or otherwise, without permission in writing from the author, except by a reviewer, who may quote brief passages in critical articles or reviews.

Illustrated by James Monroe.
Cover and interior design by JamesMonroeDesign.com.

Softcover ISBN: 979-8-9925261-0-3
Hardcover ISBN: 978-1-7350214-8-5

Printed in the United States of America
First Printing: 2024
29 28 27 26 25   5 4 3 2 1

The Greatness Zone
thegreatnesszone.com

In partnership with Wisdom/Work

For my parents and all who have the
strength, tenacity, courage and kindness to raise
great kids in a crazy world.

Contents

Introduction | ix

Laugh So You Don't Cry

Oh No! I've Turned Into My Mother! 1

Stay in Bed.. 4

Don't Interrupt Me....................................... 8

Because I Said No!...................................... 10

Grow Up and Move Out 12

My Kids Really Stink 13

More Than Me 15

Go Wash Your Hands!................................ 16

Sleep, Oh, Sleep, Where Are You???............ 18

I'll Be Alright, I'll Be Okay 22

Georgie Purcell... 24

I'll Do Better Tomorrow (The Parent's Prayer)........... 26

Love Them to The End of Time

The Things I Need You to Know 30

Blessings and Burdens 33

A Great Work in the Making 35

A Dad's Wish 37

Nighttime Sendoff 39

Bear Hug 41

Up There 44

That's Not Food. 45

A Glimpse of Me. 47

All Grown Up 49

Making the Most of My Moments

Blessed By This Mess 54

On With Life. 56

The Butterfly and The Bee 58

I Wonder 60

Friends at the Gate 62

Fashionista. 63

Go With the Flow. 65

Life's Traveling Partner 67

Between the Gaps 69

Flowers on the Table. 71

The Moodies 73

Delighted by Life. 75

The Very Best You. 77

About the Author | 79

Introduction

Parenting is not easy; I don't need to tell you that. Some days the kids are angels and we love them, and other days we would leave them out front with a sign that says, "Free, Take Me! No Questions Asked."

No matter the day, we love them intensely, care about them immensely and would do anything for them. So, maintaining our sanity, as we raise little remarkable humans, is critical.

Shared in three sections—Laugh so You Don't Cry, Love Them to the End of Time, and Making the Most of My Moments—these stories and poems were written to inspire, engage, empower and inform, to help you laugh, roll your eyes, care and relate to the universal challenges, opportunities and emotions of being a parent.

To be read alone or aloud, to your kids, for yourself or as a family, **OH, NO! I've Turned Into My Mother!** has content for every parent, stepparent, grandparent, aunt, uncle or any guardian, no matter where you are in your parenting journey.

May the rhymes entertain you, the characters inspire you and the wisdom guide you.

Stay sane and parent well,

Jay Forte

Laugh So You Don't Cry

Oh No! I've Turned Into My Mother!

I happened to notice as I shopped one day,
The things that I do and the things that I say.
Now, **who** do I think of when I act this way?
Oh no! I've become my mother today!

I clean up all spills and give toddlers a smile.
I chat with strangers for a **very** long while.
I help others find things in the right aisle.
I dress as I want, I call it **my style**.

I wipe other kids' noses when boogies do run.
I say, "Sit when you eat, or **you** are now done."
"Finish your homework, life's **not** only fun."
"Treat your things right or soon you'll have none."

I now **hear** me speak and to others I tell,
"**Don't** raise your voice, **don't** swear and **don't** yell."
"Put on clean clothes, you're beginning to smell."
"I would **gladly** be sick if that means you are well."

Oh, No! I've Turned Into My Mother!

I hear myself say, "You'll be sorry when I'm gone."
"Cover your mouth when you know you will yawn,"
"Here is my joke about a hat and a swan."
Oh dear, this mom-thing goes on and on.

I remember my mom spoke and acted this way,
I said when it's **my** turn these things **I won't** say.
The way that she acts in her weird '**momly**' way
Are now the things I **do** every day.

Yup, that's me, and I just don't know how,
When younger I'd made this very firm vow,
To be like her I would **never** allow.
But here it sure is, I'm just like her now.

I shrug and I guess that it must be this way,
We all seem to act like our parents one day.
We can fight and avoid and hope and go pray,
But still it does happen, just like they say.

Laugh So You Don't Cry

Stay in Bed

Bedtime takes 10 minutes, the **experts** all say,
They just have not been part of **my** day.

Read one long story, then even five more.
Going to bed is a tough daily chore.
"I need some water!" So I say a big "No!"
"You'll pee in your bed, and you know that is so."

But he whines and asks to leave on the light.
I smile, give a kiss and tell him good night.
I get to the door and give a long sigh
To find he's behind me, standing right by.

"Get back into bed!" I find myself say,
"I've already said this **ten** times today."
He runs back to bed and I tuck him right in,
This time he looks up with a nod and a grin.
I head through the door and out to the hall,
And find him behind me, blanket and all.

Laugh So You Don't Cry

My patience is gone. I do try, I admit,
Now angry, my angel has become a real twit.
I have **things** to get done and need him in bed,
Some clothes that need folding and things to be read.

Each bedtime I go from Jekyll to Hyde,
Mother Theresa, come and be my good guide.
Even **she** would swear when doing this chore,
Needing patience and calm and 100 things more.

Stay in Bed

Then finally all's quiet, no noise, not a wail.
I savor this moment with a hearty exhale.
I return to his room that is tidy and neat,
To find him asleep on his green dino sheet.

Tonight, now is quiet, I say an "Amen."
And I know that tomorrow it will **all** start again.
But now all is well, right now all is good.
This moment just happens the way that it should.

Two endings you choose:

Ending #1

Now tired and weary, I rub my forehead.
Glad he is quiet and asleep in his bed.
Someday I will miss these tough little bits,
These restless nights and these battles of wits.
**Then I sit on the couch, and a thought starts to sprout,
I sure will be happy when he grows up and moves out.**

Ending #2

Now tired and weary, I rub my forehead.
Glad he is quiet and asleep in his bed.
Someday I will miss these tough little bits,
These restless nights and these battles of wits.
**But I reflect back, then forget all the stress,
For he is my angel, growing into his best.**

Laugh So You Don't Cry

Don't Interrupt Me

"Mom! Mom! Mom!" It just never ends,
My son interrupts while I talk with some friends.
No patience, no manners, always in a big rush.
Though I do love him, I wish he would hush.

I've tried for what seems to be so many years
To teach this kid patience, it has me in tears.
He just goes on talking and interrupts me
When I'm busy with others, why can't he see?

He thinks he's important, he wants his own way,
Interrupting all others with something to say.
So next when it happens, to him I'll ignore,
As if I've become a closed and locked door.

Then maybe he'd get it, maybe he'd learn,
So I **don't** raise my voice or act very stern.
This he must master and so very soon,
Others won't go with his very rude tune.

I want him to be happy and succeed in his life,
To relate to all others, without any strife.
I want him to see that though we're all great,
Sometimes, with others, he'll just have to wait.

Laugh So You Don't Cry

Because I Said No!

Your son is real angry, he's so super pissed,
He's giving you the **face**.
You said "NO!" to going out in the rain,
Now he's making a mess of the place.

Your daughter's in one of her many foul moods,
Saying home is worse than at school.
You said "NO!" to lipstick at 8 years old,
She now says you're so very cruel.

Son number two is screaming and yelling,
You threw all his candy away.
You said "NO!" because it fell in the dirt,
He now says you've ruined his day.

You don't say "No!" 'cause you want to be mean,
No matter what others do say.
You say it to keep them healthy and clean,
To live so **many** more days.

So, I'll thank the goodhearted parents,
Who do so much without praise.
Who try so hard to raise them just right,
I wish I could give you a raise.

So instead, please accept my wild applause
For dealing so well with the stress.
For the way that you guide and care and support,
Preparing your kids for success.

Laugh So You Don't Cry

Grow Up and Move Out

There are times, yes there are, when I **just** can't believe
The way my kids scream and go pout.
And soon I'll be happy and very relieved
When they'll take all their stuff and move out.

Maybe I'm kidding, maybe I'm not,
It really depends on the day.
If they're kind and smart and do as they ought,
Then maybe I'll let them all stay.

My Kids Really Stink

I find that I now must **hold** my nose
When I walk in my kids' messy room.
It could be the dirty mountain of clothes,
I'm prepped with a mask and a broom.

I leaned over to kiss my oldest son Joe,
As he munched on a small piece of cake.
I was almost knocked out by his potent BO,
What a stink this kid sure can make.

My daughter, she's sweet in her mood and her smile,
There's few that are cuter than her.
But her breath can knock you out for a while,
Turn away or you'll die, that's for sure.

My Kids Really Stink

I went to the bathroom for one private minute,
I **rarely** get this any day.
I rushed back out from the **smell** that was in it,
What **do** these kids eat when they play?

When life sends its smells that bring on the stress,
I'm ready to go north or go south.
What makes me survive the stink and the mess
Is I've learned how to breathe through my mouth.

More Than Me

"She has more!" he wails as I finish to pour
The cereal, he now has thrown to the floor.
I hate when the kids all seem to keep score,
So aware of who's got even **one** more.

I say, "Focus on you, to others, ignore.
Mind your own business, I stress, I implore.
I think what I'll do if this happens once more,
Is to bring them outside, then go lock the door.

Go Wash Your Hands!

For the parents (to say to the kids):
You are loaded with tons of mean yucky germs
That come as you touch the things that go squirm,
Like your piles of fat and brown ugly worms.
Go wash your hands! About this I'm firm.

You have great friends—I think that's so nice.
If you bring home their germs, we'll **all** pay the price.
I feel I must offer this needed advice,
Go wash your hands! I won't tell you twice.

I love that you play, that's so great, that's so fine,
But please, go clean up before we all dine.
Don't complain, or mumble or even go whine,
Go wash your hands! Please follow this line.

Laugh So You Don't Cry

In this age of COVID, a mean nasty virus,
To get sick, please trust me, is not so desirous.
With germs in our noses and circling around us,
<u>Go</u> wash your hands! And, quit making a fuss.

My kids say I'm naggy because this I say,
"**Go** wash your hands to send germs far away.
This isn't to stop your fun and your play,
It's so you are well and strong every day."

For the kids (to say to the parents):
Wash up, wash up, my hands are so clean,
I got rid of the brown and rid of the green.
My hands are the cleanest they ever have been,
I did what you asked, there's no need for a scene.

Sleep, Oh, Sleep, Where Are You???

The noise and commotion, it went on all day.
Drive here, drive there, toting kids on their way.
Dead tired from moving so often and fast,
Responding to questions, each time they get asked.

So tired, can't focus, I think I could crash
On the couch or the bed in a very quick flash.
Not yet, I then think, I've got dinner to make,
I'm **so** very tired, I see my **hands** shake.

No end to this pace, it moves on and on,
Go here, go there, I feel like a pawn.
To get all this done, on this road really steep,
I need you, my friend, I need you dear Sleep.

At day's end, kids in bed, and **all** homework done,
Got through the battles, the moods and some fun.
The house is now quiet, real peace has arrived.
Time for **you** Sleep—I feel so deprived.

I dragged all day long, so weary and tired,
I need you dear Sleep, that's how I am wired.
The time is now here, to lay down and rest,
And welcome dear Sleep and end today's tests.

Laugh So You Don't Cry

I exhale and breathe and hum a short song.
Eyes closed, come on dreams, let's move this along.
But my mind starts its vicious nighttime routine,
Recounting what's wrong in my daily life scene.

"Calm down! Let it go!" I tell my crazed brain.
"To do this," I say, "just brings on the pain."
I'm now wide awake and Sleep has moved on,
It's chosen another, my Sleep friend is gone.

Sleep, Oh, Sleep, Where Are You???

Laugh So You Don't Cry

Sleep, oh Sleep, why **do** you evade?
Sleep, oh Sleep, I **wish** that you stayed.
Sleep, oh Sleep, can you **please please** return?
Sleep, dear Sleep, you're something I've earned.

Please come back and share your wonderful rest.
Please come back, I'm starting to feel renewed stress.
Don't leave me, I beg you, don't leave me right now.
I need you dear Sleep, **please** tell me how
To get you to stay, to move right on in,
To help me recharge so I **don't** need some gin.

My pleading then starts to reach a high pitch.
I close both eyes and with a small twitch
My Sleep friend returns, now calm with no mess,
My body relaxes and releases its stress.

"Tomorrow, please Sleep," I pray as I say,
"**Please** make it easy to get you to stay."
"We're on the same side, you and me, you see,
I need you dear Sleep, because others need me."

I'll Be Alright, I'll Be Okay

There will be times when life is so tough
That for **all** that you do, it seems **never** enough.
For the battles and struggles that are really rough,
For the way you can go from happy to gruff.

I'll be alright, I'll be okay,
if I can just make it through this one #!@*&%ing day.

Laugh So You Don't Cry

For the wet homework and the lost lunch.
For the call from the school about giving a punch.
For the falling lamp and the sound of its crunch.
For the dirty clothes and the mountain of grunge.

**I'll be alright, I'll be okay,
if I can just make it through this one #!@*&%ing day.**

For the fresh talk, complaining and constant rolled eyes.
For the yelling and screaming and emotional cries.
For the poking and fingers in the fresh pies.
For the tears and the sobs for not winning the prize.

**I'll be alright, I'll be okay,
if I can just make it through this one #!@*&%ing day.**

I bet if I check, there surely will be
Some traumas, some trouble, or a big whining spree.
But in that same moment, if **I** control me,
There'll also be **greatness** I know I could see.

I need to stay calm as my kids find their way,
As they learn and they grow and meet each new day.
It's not easy for them, or for me, I do say,
But I'll help them get through it, move on and not stray.

And when it gets tough, when the world's not so sweet,
I'll stop and I'll think, and then I'll repeat:
**I *will* be alright, I *will* be okay,
I know *I* can make it through *this* blessed day.**

Georgie Purcell

This is the story of young Georgie Purcell,
Whose voice was as loud as could be.
Whatever he'd tell, came out as a yell,
It was heard from the hills to the sea.

Though Georgie, our friend, was kind and was well,
His parents were just a bit miffed.
The doctor did tell, "Let him speak, don't you quell,
His strong voice is really a gift."

Day in and day out, their eardrums would swell,
It made them a little bit crazed.
Then one day we tell, our Georgie Purcell,
Went into a **new** talking phase.

Laugh So You Don't Cry

Now, **quiet** was he, when stories he'd tell,
It was **just** so pleasant to hear,
That they hugged for a spell, dear Georgie Purcell,
Then raised their voices in cheer.

He then blocked his ears, our Georgie Purcell,
And complained that the noise was extreme.
"Mom and Dad do tell what's the **deal** with the yell,
I'm right here, there's no need to scream."

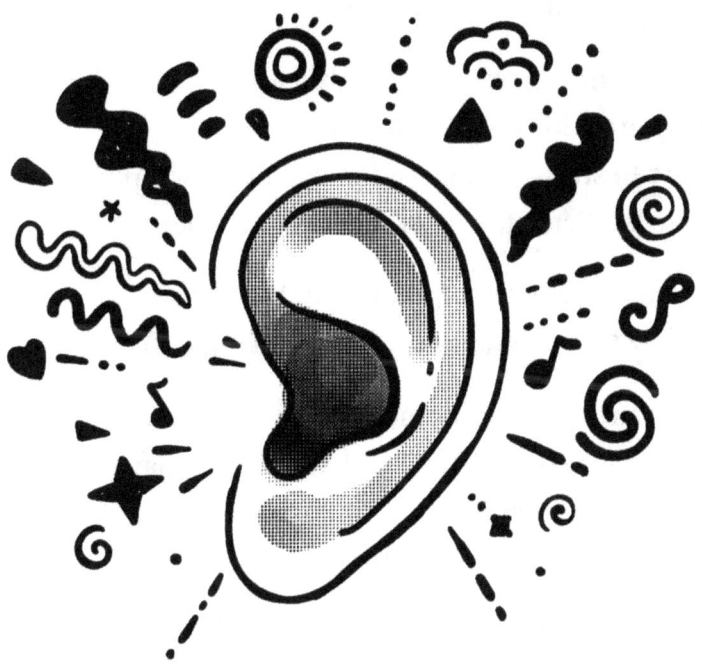

I'll Do Better Tomorrow (The Parent's Prayer)

The house is now quiet, what a night this has been,
The struggles the battles, no face with a grin.
They **don't** stay in bed, I **just** cannot win,
Now mad and upset, I think I need gin.

**I promise tomorrow, much better I'll do.
To stay so much calmer, not act like a shrew.**

I look at their faces, now finally asleep.
Really great kids, I just love them a heap.
They **can** stress me out and make me go weep.
Please let them stay quiet, not even one peep.

**I promise tomorrow, much better I'll do.
To stay so much calmer, no throwing a shoe.**

I look through their homework and see what they say
About their young lives that happen each day.
I smile to see they are finding their way.
I need to be patient, I ask that I may.

**I promise tomorrow, much better I'll do.
To stay so much calmer, I need this breakthrough.**

Laugh So You Don't Cry

I offer small thoughts at day's-end oh so rough,
To not get all twisted 'bout meaningless stuff.
To never be mean or hurtful or gruff.
To help them along when they find their days tough.

**I promise tomorrow, much better I'll do.
I'll stay focused on blessings that come into view.**

Love Them to The End of Time

The Things I Need You to Know

It is **real** tough, this parenting role,
Without clear guidance or rules.
But I move **on** ahead with my critical goal,
To teach you important life tools.

There are **some** things, I need you to know,
That I share with you from my heart.
The things that will help you be great and glow,
So you're ready for life from the start.

I know my role as your mom or your dad
Is to guide and not tell you the way.
So, here's a few things I need you to have
As you start each one of your days.

First, know yourself, and **what** makes you great,
Your abilities, talents and gifts.
These will help you find your right place,
Then in life you won't go adrift.

Next, you are here to **more** than survive,
This world—you're here to improve.
Find what helps you live and to thrive,
Think wisely, then go make your move.

Love Them to The End of Time

Be kind every day, in all that you do,
Being kind improves your whole life.
See others as just as important as you,
And your life will have much less strife.

There's still so much more I just want to share
So you **have** a life that you love.
See how often I guide and I care,
So your life fits you like a glove.

Communicate open and honest and clear,
Tell the truth and always stand tall.
Be **yourself** at school and in your career,
Get back up when life makes you fall.

The Things I Need You to Know

Accept yourself, just as you are,
Do the same with all of your brothers.
You **have** what it takes to go very far,
While supporting and helping all others.

Ignore petty actions and any mean words
That will come from here and from there.
Tune them out, pretend they've never been heard,
Move on and don't give them a care.

The world can be mean, not sure why that is,
But be ready for all that it sends.
Life can feel like a sudden pop quiz,
That tests who you think are your friends.

Stay strong, stay alert, but mostly I say
Be kind, care deeply and share.
These words will help you find your own way
In the world you discover out there.

I'm here as your guide, to make sense of it all,
I've been on this road once before.
Please heed my wise words, to go and stand tall,
So you'll have a life you adore.

Blessings and Burdens

So, what do you say to your kids as they find
That life can be tough, it's just not that kind?
How can you help them find joy and be strong
When things in their life, to them, can feel wrong?

I **don't** have the answer, but I **do** have a thought,
Share **this** when they seem in a really tough spot:

> In life each day, you'll find some of both,
> The blessings and burdens, they're part of your growth.
> You can't have a life with only just one,
> They come as a pair, that's how life is done.
>
> Let's start with the blessings, as this is the way
> To focus on great things that happen each day.
> They give you a boost, they amp up your soul,
> They bring you great joy, no matter your role.
>
> Watch for the blessings you find everywhere,
> They help you do life with grace and with flair.
> They add daily value, they help you to thrive
> When struggles and challenges start to arrive.

Blessings and Burdens

Now all sorts of burdens will show up in life,
Some may just cut like the blade of a knife.
Others are small, still are hurtful and mean,
They make your days dull; life loses its sheen.

So why do we get these—the burdens and pain,
The challenge and loss and feelings of blame?
In these tough moments—that's where you find growth,
Learning the things you're needing the most.

Done well, your burdens are something you master.
From burdens to blessings, you move along faster.
You learn and you grow, you get better each day,
You turn tough things to great things you find on the way.

That's just how life is, don't fight it, move on.
Roll with the punches, that's how you get strong.
Both blessings and burdens, each day will arrive,
Be grateful for both, that means you're alive.

A Great Work in the Making

You want great behavior, and then they just won't.
You want some real kindness and then they just don't.
What **is** the problem, I just have to ask,
Why kids can't complete the most simple of tasks?

But to be fully human, is **no** easy feat.
Remember way back when **you** weren't so sweet.
It takes practice and time and someone to guide,
So they can find **who** they are deep inside.

They are, like you, a great work in the making.
This takes much care like a bread you are baking.
Think of fine art and the time that it took,
Like the colors of paint or the words in a book.

In life we're not born with a manual or guide
Of how to be **us** with a world view so wide.
For that we must learn, a little each day;
Small careful steps as we move on our way.

Be patient, be kind, they're all learning how
To be who they are, to be their best now.
Now, cut them some slack when they act as they do,
It just takes some time for their best to come through.

A Great Work in the Making

So, don't let them think, **not once** in a day
That **they are not loved** by the things that you say.
Your words have such power, much more than you know,
To help or to hurt, as they all start to grow.

To parent is tough, it's a really hard job.
It can give you great pains and a head that will throb.
But be fair and supporting, be loving and kind,
Be open and honest, and soon you will find
That they will then **get it**, they'll **learn** the right things,
To find their own way as the grow their own wings.

Take a big breath when you're feeling so crazed.
Work to stay calm and refocus on praise.
Soon they'll arrive and they'll be **so** less errant,
And then comes their turn to go be a parent.

A Dad's Wish

It's no easy job, to be a great dad,
There's work and worries and times that you're mad.
There isn't a book or a guide or a map
That helps you be strong and not break or not snap.
It takes time and focus and even some luck
To inspire your kids when you feel like you're stuck.

My advice, if you ask, is to be ready to say,
Your wishes for each kid as they **go** through their days.

A Dad's Wish

My Wishes for You

 I wish you are happy, to know who you are,
To learn to dream big so you'll go very far.

I wish you to read all the books that you can,
To learn to think deeply and have a life plan.

I wish you to care for yourself and for others,
And always respect your siblings and mother.

I wish you to know that you're here for a reason,
And I'll help you to find it no matter the season.

I wish you to know it's your job to improve
The things all around you—you make the first move.

I wish you to care about all that you see,
From people to air to oceans to trees.

I wish you to have a love that is real,
And always embrace the way that you feel.

I wish you to be kind and honest and true,
But what I wish most? Go be the best you.

Though I may wish these, I still **do** know
That **you** make this happen, this is **your** show.
I'm here to guide, to teach and to share,
So, you're ready to be in the big world out there.

Nighttime Sendoff

Good night, good night, I say with a smile,
It's been quite a day, you've been up for a while.
Now we slow down, we get ready to rest,
When tomorrow arrives, we'll be at our best.

Here is a **thought** as we slow down tonight,
And get ourselves settled and turn down the lights.
Let's **now** go back and think on our day,
And give a big **thanks** for what came our way.

Share what you are grateful for today...

Nighttime Sendoff

With tomorrow we'll get another new start
To do some great things, that come from our heart.
Let's think and imagine what things we can do
To improve something old or make something new.

Share what you want to happen tomorrow...

We're almost done now with our off-to-bed time.
There's just one more thing to do in this rhyme.
We sleep so much better when think of a theme
Of something we love, a **go-to-sleep** dream.

Share what you want to dream about tonight...

Good night, my sweet, here's my strong hug,
With good thoughts and dreams, under covers so snug.
Rest well, sleep tight so you're ready to be
Part of the great things tomorrow we'll see.

Good night. XO

Bear Hug

Every morning and every night, the father would give his three girls a **bear hug**. Holding them with his strong arms, he would say, "My cubs, this hug is to let you know how much I love you. I circle you with my strength to keep you safe, now and even when we are not together. It will always be there for you—now and forever." This made them feel safe, secure and loved.

As with all children, they quickly grew up—school, friends, activities and sports. He watched them develop into smart, attractive, kind, caring and remarkable people. He lovingly watched as they each worked hard to find their own way.

Bear Hug

No matter the distance, the father spoke to his daughters every day; sometimes they would visit, sometimes it would be a call. They always talked about life, relationships, careers, loves and hurts—all the things that matter. At the end of each visit or a call, the father would say 'bear hug.' They each always knew he was there for them—caring, loving and supportive. It was always that way.

But life is not forever. And soon the father grew older, his health failing. Brought to the hospital, knowing the end of his life was near, he was soon joined by his three girls, together, just as when they were young.

He looked at each of the three with admiration—impressed by who they had become. Each was confident, happy and loving, now established with families of her own. He smiled at them. They knew the smile—it was the smile that they had seen all these years—a smile of tenderness and support—a smile of encouragement and concern—a timeless smile—a father's smile.

He reached out his hand—they all held it. He squeezed with his fading energy, feeling the warmth and softness of their skin. He was flooded with memories of their lives—as babies, children, teenagers and adults. He held their hands, remembering all that he could about their lives. He wanted the moment to last—he wanted to freeze time—to have this one moment remain forever. But that, unfortunately, is not how life is. They felt his grip weaken—their eyes connected. He did his best job to wink and smile as he always had, then whispered, 'bear hug.'

Love Them to The End of Time

They each held his hand until he no longer held theirs. They placed his frail hand gently on his chest and each gave him a kiss—"Sleep well Dad—it was your hugs that kept us safe and reminded us how much we were loved. It will always be."

That evening, each of the girls sat with their children. "Let me tell you a story," each one said. "We call it Bear Hug."

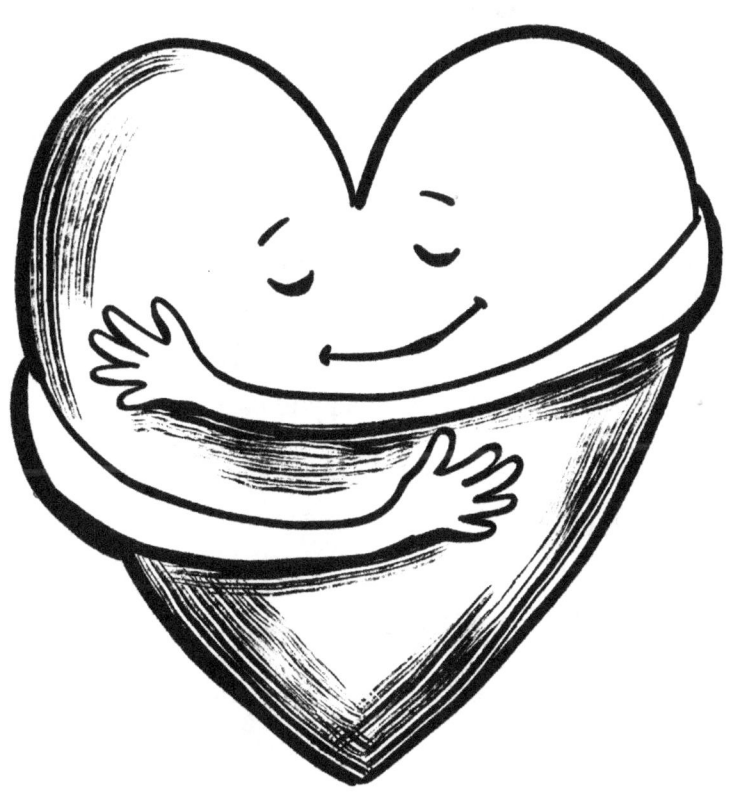

Up There

You got tired of walking, you started to cry,
So I place you way up on my shoulders so high.
The world can look different from your place in the sky,
Up there on my shoulders you feel you can fly.

So we walked and we talked, in your high shoulders' chair.
A space just for you, this space that I share
To help you see more, to become more aware
Of life's great adventures you see from up there.

Soon you will grow, and no longer you'll ride
High up on my shoulders, now you'll walk by my side.
We'll still have adventures in our world big and wide.
No matter your age, I'm always your guide.

That's Not Food

We're all in a rush to get something to eat,
Food nowadays seems like nothing but treats.
But food is for health, for growing up strong.
Good food is needed for a life to be long.

Not junk, not garbage, not sugary things,
But real food, the things that a great garden brings.
Not packaged, not processed, real food is the key
To live well and healthy, the best life can be.

**Teach them all early to do their own part,
To learn about food and eat really smart.**

A great skill for a life is to learn how to cook.
Use a neighbor, a download, or even a book.
Teach them to boil and sauté and bake,
And eat as they should and good things they will make.

That's Not Food

From time I was six, my mom said to me,
"Your health's up to you, with the cooking from me.
But soon you will learn to cook and sauté,
So you'll always eat right, no matter the day."

We'd ask for some snacks, the ones from the store,
But high-processed foods never entered our door.
"That's just not food!" my mom would then say.
"Those things will not keep you healthy today."

**Teach them all early to do their own part,
To learn about food and eat really smart.**

Sure, there are some things that taste really great
But do nothing for health, they just add to your waist.
Remember that food is here to give you
A good life, a strong life, so your health will shine through.

**Teach them all early to eat really smart,
And for life you'll prepare them to do their own part.**

A Glimpse of Me

I heard the big clunk, my son's shoes on the stairs,
I looked over my shoulder to see,
A glimpse that **this** moment **did** choose to share,
Seeing him, is like looking at me.

The nose and the chin, the hair and the eyes,
That's me, not so long ago.
Drifting along with my head in the sky,
Just fine to go with the flow.

I sometimes get miffed that he's not very clear
About where in life he is going.
Then I do see there's **no** need for fear,
He's just getting started with growing.

A Glimpse of Me

It took me a while, my folks also said
To find which way was for me.
So I smile as he snacks on a handful of bread,
Dropping crumbs that ants meet with glee.

"Hey," I call out, "You're making a mess."
I say in my nagging dad style.
He then shrugs at me like I'm being a pest,
But then cleans it up with a smile.

Once done, he goes to play right outside,
With his silly and big goofy grin.
I love to see him take things in stride
With a smile from his eyes to his chin.

He's a good kid, and I was one too,
I remember this fact quite well.
So I go back to watching this wonderful view,
And my heart, with pride, does swell.

All Grown Up

I held their hands when they were so small.
I helped them to move as they learned to crawl.
I wiped the tears when they hurt their knees.
I helped them to climb way up in the trees.

I changed all their diapers and dealt with the smell.
I stayed in their room when they didn't feel well.
I cuddled and sang to them night after night,
To help them feel safe and to chase away fright.

I walked them to school and met at the door,
To share in their day, was never a chore.
I drove them to soccer with meals in the car,
I went to their games some near and some far.

I helped them to read great stories each night.
I helped them to dream by a campfire light.
I helped them to find out what makes their heart sing.
We spoke about life and all that it brings.

All Grown Up

I listened to wishes and wild-eyed dreams.
I cried with them when they were cut from the team.
I helped them prepare for a really tough test.
I gave them great hugs when they felt really stressed.

My heart beats with theirs, we're connected as one,
I **do truly** care 'bout their troubles and fun.
I think of them always, each moment, each day,
I love to know what they think and they say.

But grow as they do, it's life's strangest thing,
To make you grow close, then to arm them with wings.
They need to move on, to find their own way,
To live their own lives, to run their own days.

They don't need me now, they're okay on their own.
I helped them prepare each day as they've grown.
But here I feel sad, as it now seems for me
That my children, my loves, so want to be free.

Love Them to The End of Time

I know I've prepared them to be wise and strong.
I know that my role was to help them belong.
And now they can live on their own, and that's great.
I knew this would come, but so fast, can't it wait?

I wanted more time to hold them real tight.
I wanted more moments to keep them in sight.

I wanted more time to see those big eyes.
I wanted more moments to share all their highs.

I wanted more time camped out on the chair.
I wanted more moments of being right there.

I wanted more time with laughter and songs.
I wanted more moments to take them along.

I wanted more time of chatting and talking.
I wanted more moments of quietly walking.

I wanted more time of cheering them on.
I wanted more pictures on the fridge that were drawn.

But I **do** really know that my job and my role
Was to help them to grow up and be fully whole.
And now at this point, I should **feel** really blessed,
I'm sad 'cause I miss them, my heart feels this stress.

So, **I'll** call my friends and keep moving, I say.
I'll rethink how I'll fill each one of my days.
I do miss them, my kids, as they're now on their own.
But here in my heart, they know they are home.

Making the Most of My Moments

Blessed By This Mess

We expect that if we act really kind,
Good things around us, is what we will find.
If we're caring and loving, and also act just,
Then good things will happen, on that we can trust.

As a country, a city, a family and school,
Do good and do well, should be the gold rule.
But instead what we find in most every day,
Complaints and problems that don't go away.

A warming planet, pandemic and strife,
Hate crimes and assaults that cut like a knife.
Meanness and fighting—a continual stress,
Life always seems in some kind of mess.

So, what if this 'mess' had a message that we
Could see that it gives us a way to be free?
The **mess** shows us things that are needing some work,
Like learning to be kind and less of a jerk.

Making the Most of My Moments

We are blessed by our mess, remember this now.
Our mess shows us **where**, so we can choose **how**
To make things much better, to always improve
Each moment, each day, each thing that we do.

Said Mencius, a philosopher, and truly wise man,
Don't be upset if things **don't** go as planned.
Though we want things to go in our way,
When they don't, it just makes room for some play.

The strife and the messes are just a reminder
There's room to improve, if we take off the blinder.
Each mess has a lesson important to teach,
To expand what we know and increase our reach.

The messes can share where there's something to gain,
Calm down, think it through and use your big brain.
Focus your thoughts on what **else** can be done,
Go solve, don't vent, and you'll hit a home run.

Something **great** you can make out of something not so;
The mess and the challenge are where you can grow.
So greet them and bless them, don't focus on loss.
The value will always be so worth the cost.

On With Life

You read the headlines and all the news,
There always seems more wrong than right.
Things seem so heavy and loaded with blues,
And always something to fight.

But that is just life, it comes at you fast,
It comes like a racing freight train.
But **you've** what it takes to succeed and get past
And find sun when it seems like just rain.

On with life! you say, as the challenges show,
You smile as you meet every hurt.
On with life! you say, let the strong winds go blow,
You'll make diamonds from all your packed dirt.

On with life! you say, as you have a tough day,
With challenge both heavy and strong.
On with life! you say, 'cause it's better that way,
You've got strength to last all day long.

Making the Most of My Moments

On with life! you say, as you notice the good,
And the things that make you go smile.
On with life! you say, you do as you should,
You meet life with your own special style.

No matter the moment, there'll always be strife,
You'll find challenge and all sorts of stress.
In each of these moments say, "On with my life!"
And each day you'll always feel blest.

The Butterfly and The Bee

A large yellow and orange butterfly named Flo landed on a beautiful purple lilac flower. Sitting in the sun, drinking the sweet lavender nectar, Flo smiled. Then, a big black and yellow bee, they all call him Butch, flew right into Flow and pushed her off the purple flower.

Still smiling, she fluttered on to another darker purple lilac flower, one that was even more fragrant. On this new flower, Flo not only smiled but started humming. Feeling each of the sun's warm rays, Flo burst into song. Butch followed her and again, pushed her off the fragrant flower. Flo, still smiling and singing, fluttered around and gently landed on a small blue and yellow pansy that grew close to the ground.

Digg, the chipmunk who lived in the stone wall at the edge of the garden, watched as Butch, the bully bee, pushed Flo from flower to flower. Scurrying over to Flo, Digg frowned, looked up and quietly asked Flo, "I have to ask—why aren't you upset by that bully bee, Butch, the way he keeps pushing you off the flowers?"

Flo stopped singing and smiled at Digg. She noticed his dark eyes and beautiful smooth fur. She loved his whiskers and how his nose twitched when he spoke.

Making the Most of My Moments

"Digg," she said, never stopping her smile, "look how many flowers there are in this garden. They are all so beautiful. If I can't stay on one, I'll go find another. And each one is just a bit different in the way it looks and tastes. Everywhere I land is a gift, and I am happy to be here. I always focus on being happy and never let the actions of others take away my happiness."

Digg's thought for a moment, then shifted his frown to a smile. He too was happy to live near this wonderful garden. Flo fluttered around Digg's head, sharing a butterfly's version of a hug, and flew off smiling and singing. Digg's smile lasted all day, and some say they heard him hum.

I Wonder

Out for a ride, along the bike trail,
On a day that is warm and real nice.
I notice the people, some tanned and some pale,
And wonder about all their lives.

Are they happy, are they loved, how is their day?
I wonder as I ride right on by.
What do they do to move in their way,
What kind of things do they try?

What are their hobbies? What makes their lives grand?
I wonder as I ride right on by.
Do they show up each day with a focus and plan,
And give things their very best try?

What things excite them and help them feel great?
I wonder as I ride right on by.
What joyous times do they have with their mates?
Do they love the woods and the sky?

What work do they do as they show up each day?
I wonder as I ride right on by.
What fears do they face that they **must** send away,
To shift from the downs to the highs?

What makes them happy and what makes them glad?
I wonder as I ride right on by.
How much of the time are they mad or are sad,
Does our mean world make them go cry.

Making the Most of My Moments

What makes them kind and so very caring?
I wonder as I ride right on by.
With the people around them whose lives they are sharing,
What joys go make their hearts fly?

All of this happens as I ride on my bike,
And pass so many on the trail.
I wonder what all of their lives are like,
And wish them calm winds and no gales.

I **can't** make their lives the way that I'd like,
That's just not for me to go do.
But **I** can help out with a smile as I bike,
And improve this moment's life view.

Friends at the Gate

It's almost noon, hurry, don't wait.
Our friends have arrived, they're here at the gate.
They get so impatient, they hate when we're late.
They act like real jerks when they get in this state.

I pause and think, these friends are **not** great.
They whine and complain and then they berate.
Then I just think, I don't care if they wait,
I'm going back in, they can stay at the gate.

Fashionista

There was a time, not so long ago,
I was hip and cool, a regular joe.
My clothes and my style, my unique way of dressing,
Some say it's a gift, maybe even a blessing.

My clothes followed trends—the sites did suggest
Of the suits and the shirts of the very-well-dressed.
Of the jeans and the shoes and the hats and coats,
I shared all the fashions, the very high notes.

But then time moved on and now I do see
My grandfather's face looking right back at me.
My redish plaid pants and my green checkered shirt,
No longer the combo that inspires the flirt.

I now see more folks rolling their eyes
When they see what I wear, a look they despise.
But, who cares, I think. **I** dress to feel good,
Not dressing the way **they** think that I should.

Comfortable, casual and practical I say,
Is how I choose to get dressed every day.
Gone is the need to be chic or highbrow,
Clothes should be practical, this I've learned now.

So complain if you want, all you hipsters and critics,
Just wait till you're older and a little arthritic.
Zippers and buttons need fingers so strong,
With Velcro and snaps, you'll never go wrong.

Go With the Flow

We always want things to go in our way.
And people to do what we ask and we say.
But sometimes they don't, you know this is true.
Then, "go with the flow," is a good phrase for you.

As a parent, sometimes you surely will see
That your patience wears thin, I know you'll agree.
If you stay in the feelings of mad, sad and stress,
You'll make for yourself a really big mess.

Go with the flow means you just let things be,
Don't react—stay calm—and new options you'll see.
To do this is harder than most people think,
To act sane and calm when you're pushed to the brink.

Go With the Flow

So here are two things I find that **I** use,
When my kids seem to bring the stress and the blues:

> The first—take a breath then let it out slow.
> When you take a deep breath, it makes you say "Whoa!"
> Slow down, see things clearly, to see what you know.
> As you go with the flow, your options will grow.

> The second—I say is a joke you should bring.
> A laugh is so great to move past a sting.
> It's hard to be mad when a smile's your thing.
> As you go with the flow, it will help your heart sing.

That's what I have for some words of advice
To move from all crazed to someone more nice.
Relax, let it fly, life's like this you see,
To **go with the flow** is a wise way to be.

Life's Traveling Partner

In the light or the dark
Of days or of moods,
You are there—solid, present, loving.

In the struggles and the joys
Of work and of life,
You are there—solid, present, loving.

In the fun and the fury
Of adventures and challenges,
You are there—solid, present, loving.

In the noise and the quiet
Of in crowds or alone,
You are there—solid, present, loving.

In the health and the illness
In each moment of life,
You are there—solid, present, loving.

In the dreams and the fears
Of growing and aging,
You are there—solid, present, loving.

Life's Traveling Partner

In the care and the frustration
Of sharing the daily space,
You are there—solid, present, loving.

In the worries and the pride
Of raising great kids,
You are there—solid, present, loving.

In the better and the worse
Of life's daily moments,
You are there—solid, present, loving.

How are my days better?
With you in each one—for life—
Solid, present and loving.

Between the Gaps

Our minds are so noisy, filled with the chatter
Of things that we feel and think that they matter.
If we think it, it's important, it's something we knew,
To us, all our thoughts are **factually true**.

But a thought is a thought, nothing more, nothing less.
It can lead us to peace, or it can bring on some stress.
When we realize that thoughts are just fleeting sparks,
We can let them soar by without leaving their marks.

For in our small thoughts, we see only us,
Our world, **our** lives—that's **all** we discuss.
The same things, repeated, we constantly see,
Our thoughts script the world "according to me."

Between the Gaps

But what is important to become most aware
Is between all our thoughts is more than just air.
Between all our thoughts is the space that we need
To access our wisdom, the wisdom that feeds
Our connection to greatness, to ideas more divine,
To go and solve things with solutions so fine.

That space is real quiet, no noisy 'our-thoughts.'
There's room to discover, to connect all the dots.
There's space to tune in to our inner deep knowing,
To access ideas that never stop showing.

When we **slow** down our thoughts, **we** then create space,
We access a place that few of us face.
We connect into wisdom that comes from all ages,
We tap into thinking to guide our life's stages.

Take a minute, be quiet. Be still. Be aware.
Slow the mind down, you can if you dare.
Move past your thoughts, to access that space
That shares its wisdom and knowledge with grace.

Flowers on the Table

Life should be celebrated, no matter the day.
It's more **how you think** than **what** comes your way.
It's your choice to see what's great around you,
To celebrate each moment as fresh and as new.

It's been said by some for so many years,
To always do extra, this approach you will hear.
For sure, you can get by just doing enough,
But to make things feel special, it's just not that tough.

Now, start to go notice the things that add grace
That make your world better, that add to your space.
Like flowers on the table when it's time to go eat,
Like cloth napkins and music, to make dining a treat.

Flowers on the Table

Notice your space, at work and at home.
Go look at each one, stay focused, don't roam.
Walk through your space, think, "What can I do
To make each one better, to improve what I view?"

The moment is now, let me be really clear,
What could improve in what you find here?
It's the difference from having dessert with plain cake,
And one with rich frosting or one that you baked.

We **get** in a rut and go through the motions,
We miss out on life, getting lost in commotions.
So make time each day to add just one thing
To make your space great, to make your space sing.
Then you will see when you do things this way,
You've found the key to a remarkable day.

The Moodies

When things go all wrong, they go this way, not that.
They get you upset and you act like a brat.
You say mean things, and you don't act so kind.
The more you get angry, the more anger you'll find.

You're not alone when it comes to this scene,
We all get the moodies and act really mean.
When things don't go right, we have feelings of mad,
And then what we do can make others feel sad.

Moodies, we **hate** them, we **don't** feel too great.
In fact, it's a feeling that most of us hate.
When troubles arrive or blocks come your way,
The moodies can bring out the bad things you say.

The Moodies

So what do you do, when you notice they're here,
You're in a big moodie, that's so very clear?
How do you stop it from making a mess?
How can you shift from this moment of stress?

It's been said that we all have a choice
To control our emotions and use our own voice.
Though things may upset you, we know this is true,
How you go act will be up to just you.

Need ideas? Try this—you have to get moving,
Trust me on this, it's something I'm proving.
Go stand up and shake, or do a small dance,
Or act like a statue that is holding its stance.

You can sing or can hum, to clear your own mind
Of the meanest of moodies that you seem to find.
Or, make up new words and say them aloud
To send all those moodies up into the clouds.

You can wave both arms and give a head nod,
Or make up a poem 'bout some guy named Todd.
You can stomp your feet to help them be gone,
Or make up new words to a favorite song.

I hope you see what's going on here—
You stopped the mean moodies by shifting a gear.
You moved your mind to something less crazed
To help you be better in each of your days.

Delighted by Life

It has been said that each day brings a blessing
When we show up without all the stressing.
For that we must learn to focus on good,
To do what we can and to act as we should.

Habits are strong to build and release,
Some you should keep and some you should cease.
Think of the times you go and find fault,
And spend all your time in fear and assault.

What if instead, a new habit you make,
One with a focus on things that are great.
Be impressed by the things the world with you shares,
Be impressed by the people and life you find there.

Delighted by Life

It's **your** choice to spend your moments in frowns,
To focus on lack and all sorts of downs.
Or shift to a focus that raises you up
With things that engage you and fill your life's cup.

Be thrilled by your day, find things that excite,
Don't let the stresses take hold and burn bright.
In each of your moments, it's you who can choose
To be delighted by life, not stuck in the blues.

The Very Best You

You are not on the planet to simply exist,
You have a **much** larger role.
You are **here** to add **your** unique twist,
In the process, become fully whole.

Down deep inside, in each one of us,
Is a hero who passes all tests.
Find that great self—your deep inner plus,
That makes what you touch be its best.

We **each** are born great, that is the truth,
But that's up to us to go find.
We use each day that begins in our youth,
To allow that greatness to shine.

You are born with **bold and great** gifts,
We **all** are, so let them come through.
They guide your way, so you don't go adrift,
They bring out the very best you.

The Very Best You

The world is waiting for you to go raise,
That thing that makes you unique.
Then bring it to every one of your days,
To live the life that you seek.

Pass on these thoughts as a mom or a dad
To your kids as they meet life and grow.
To be their best selves makes a life that is glad,
And brings joy wherever they go.

About the Author

Passionate to help others discover, develop and live what is best in them, to be ready for great and amazing lives, Jay Forte, a certified executive coach, educator, author and family poet, shares important life lessons in all he writes.

Growing up in a large Italian family, raising three daughters, actively engaging with eight grandchildren and supporting organizations and dynamic workplaces, have provided Jay with endless wisdom and humor that inspires his stories and poems. Life is truly a comedian and our best teacher—we must laugh as we learn each day.

Jay has created the "Let's Activity Together" series, a collection of interactive activity books, and the "Let's Read Together" series, a collection of interactive stories and poems, to help families imagine, create, communicate and spend time together, away from technology. Jay is also the author of numerous poetry books and **The Greatness Zone—Know Yourself, Find Your Fit, Transform the World**, an important life resource to teach everyone how to find their place in today's world.

Passionate about words and rhyme, his work has been called "profound, funny, entertaining and wise—a modern poet." And, as a caring coach, dad and grampie, he always encourages kids and parents to expand their creativity, imagination, focus on adventure and personal contribution.

When not helping people to be their best, build stronger family bonds, solve challenges and learn how to do their part to make a better world, Jay writes, gardens and cooks, spending time with his big family in both New England and the Florida Keys.

To see more of Jay's family and children-based books, collections and resources, go to TheGreatnessZone.com

About the Illustrator

James Monroe is an experienced illustrator and graphic designer with over 18 years of expertise in creating captivating visuals for books, collaborating closely with authors and publishers to bring their stories to life. Known for his versatile style and keen eye for detail, James has developed a reputation for his ability to seamlessly blend traditional and digital techniques, crafting illustrations that resonate with audiences of all ages. His portfolio includes a diverse range of projects, from children's books to complex graphic novels, showcasing his talent for storytelling through art. Passionate about visual communication, James is dedicated to enhancing narratives with his unique artistic vision, making him a sought-after professional in the publishing industry.

Please visit jamesmonroedesign.com

The Books of Wisdom/Work

Wisdom/Work is a new cooperative, cutting edge imprint and resource for publishing and offering books by practical philosophers and innovative thinkers that provide a positive cultural impact, the best of ancient and modern wisdom with guidance for all to be ready for life at every stage. When we do the inner wisdom work, it elevates our experience.

A primary focus of the Wisdom/Work imprint is to make available high-quality content with expedited production and release and expanded benefits to authors, filling the broad publication gap between the scholarly world of university press books that are focused on academic concerns and the fast-paced world of major trade publishers, focused mainly on profit. By encouraging and supporting authors to develop and share practical wisdom for all ages and stages of life around the themes of success, ethics, happiness, meaning, purpose, partnership, the nature of good work, the many shapes of fulfilling adventure, and how best to live a good life in our time, the Wisdom/Work imprint provides a greater reader experience, practical life-success wisdom, and affordability for book buyers.

The imprints of Wisdom/Work and The Greatness Zone work in partnership to provide engaging, informative, and practical wisdom-based books for today's younger audiences and families.

For inquiries into our current and future publishing plans, to become acquainted with all Wisdom/Work books or to purchase books at a bulk discount, please inquire through the website of the founder and editor in chief, Tom Morris, TomVMorris.com. For more information about the books of The Greatness Zone, see TheGreatnessZone.com.

www.ingramcontent.com/pod-product-compliance
Lightning Source LLC
Chambersburg PA
CBHW080447110426
42743CB00016B/3301